JOURNEY FOR THE PLANET

A Kid's Five Week Adventure to Create an Earth-friendly Life

David Gershon

Published by Empowerment Institute
ISBN 978-0-9644373-0-2
Copyright © 1994, 2007 David Gershon
Printed in Canada

Second Edition
9 8 7 6 5 4 3 2

Empowerment Institute
P.O. Box 428
Woodstock, New York 12498
www.empowermentinstitute.net

This book is printed on 100% post consumer waste Forest Stewardship Certified recycled paper, using plant-based inks. The paper is processed chlorine free and manufactured using biogas energy.

By using 100% post consumer waste recycled paper instead of virgin fibers, this edition saved:

Tree(s): 33
Solid waste: 2,072lb
Water: 19,561gal
Suspended particles in the water: 13.1lb
Air emissions: 4,551lb
Natural gas: 4,743ft^3

This book is dedicated to you for answering the call to heal our planet.

ACKNOWLEDGMENTS

I wish to offer special thanks to the following people. Steve Connolly for his research assistance and thinking partnership in the first edition of this book. Dan Wetzel for his charming and wondrous illustrations. Doug Hines for his captivating graphic design. Eve Baer for her constant support in program development. Laurie Schwartz for stewarding this program with teachers throughout the country. Steve Busch for his skillful graphic design assistance in developing the second edition of this book. Gail Straub, my dear wife, for encouraging my child self to express itself. Lastly, I wish to thank the thousands of children who have participated in this program and inspired us all!

TABLE OF CONTENTS

THE JOURNEY

You are about to go on an amazing journey—one that will help you and the planet. It will be fun, challenging and exciting. Over a five week period you will learn how to take action to use our Earth's precious and limited natural resources with greater care. Your efforts to live an Earth-friendly life will help make sure there are enough resources so that others can live their lives now and in the future. It will also help you become part of the global warming solution. Each week of the journey, you will meet an animal guide who will offer special knowledge to help you.

Earthy, a friendly earthworm, will be your guide on the first part of your journey called, "Dumping on Garbage." A playful and fun-loving frog named Pondsy will be your guide and companion for the second part, "Wasting Water is All Wet." Sky, the eagle, has seen a lot and will share some ancient knowledge with you in the third part of your journey, "Getting a Charge Out of Saving Energy." The fourth part of your adventure, "Good Buys Are Forever," is guided by Munk, a busy little chipmunk who's always running around. In the final part of your journey, "Watch Out Planet, Here I Come!," a wise dolphin named Magic will guide you in teaching others how to help the planet.

To make your adventure more fun, invite a friend to join you. Your friend and you can form your own "EcoTeam!" Having someone to talk to about your successes and challenges will make your journey more enjoyable and rewarding.

Have a great journey. The planet is counting on you!

INSTRUCTIONS FOR GOING ON THE JOURNEY

1. Read all the actions in the part of the Journey you are about to take and decide which ones you want to do. Each action has a point value which helps you know how much effort is required. A one point action is easier or saves less resources than a two or three point action. If you want to achieve Global Hero status, you need to take enough actions to equal the required point total for that section.

2. Decide on the actions you will do. Then enter the day and time you will do each action on your travel log in the column: "Action Plan."

3. Show your action plan to your parent(s) so they are aware of what you are doing and can give you suggestions. Check off on your travel log when you have done this in the column "Shown to Parent(s)."

4. After you have done each action, check it off on your travel log in the "Action Done" column.

5. When you complete each part of the Journey, total the points you have earned and enter it at the bottom of that section of the travel log where it says "Global Hero Points Earned." You're now ready to move on. Repeat steps 1-5 for each part of the journey.

That's it! Have fun as you help improve life on our planet for yourself, other kids, parent(s), animals and all the plants and trees.

Thanks for caring and taking this journey for the planet.

OH, CHECK THIS OUT!

JOURNEY FOR THE PLANET

ADVENTURE THIS WAY

DUMPING ON GARBAGE—TRAVEL LOG

Actions	Action Plan		Shown to Parent(s)	Action Done	Points
No Garbage Lunches	Day:	Time:	☐	☐	3
Bag Bags	Day:	Time:	☐	☐	1
Wipe Swipe	Day:	Time:	☐	☐	1
Gesundheit!	Day:	Time:	☐	☐	1
If Your Eyes Are Bigger Than Your Stomach	Day:	Time:	☐	☐	2
Let It Rot	Day:	Time:	☐	☐	3
Every Little Bit Helps	Day:	Time:	☐	☐	3
Artist at Work	Day:	Time:	☐	☐	1
Trash or Treasure	Day:	Time:	☐	☐	3
Back by Popular Demand	Day:	Time:	☐	☐	3
Relating to Nature: Branching Out	Day:	Time:	☐	☐	1

Points Needed: 12   Global Hero Points Earned ☐

DUMPING ON GARBAGE

YOUR GUIDE: THE EARTHWORM

I am Earthy, your guide for the first part of your journey, "Dumping on Garbage." Why should you listen to me?, you may ask. The reason is that I am one of nature's best recyclers! I eat up bits of garbage and turn them into fresh soil. I would like to share with you what I know about living an Earth-friendly lifestyle.

Humans throw away tons of garbage every day. The sad part is that there is no such place as "away." If you think about it, your garbage has not gone "away," it has only been taken to someplace out of your sight. People need to change their throw-away habits.

The Earth's recycle creatures, like me, cannot keep up with all the garbage, and that's not good. Each person needs to learn to reduce the amount of garbage he or she personally creates. This part of the Journey will help you do that.

NO GARBAGE LUNCHES

WHY ACT? If your throwaway habits are like those of most kids, the garbage you send to a landfill every year takes up a space big enough to park a small car in! Much of this comes from your school lunch, picnic trash, or snacks at a friend's house. Plastic wrappers you throw "away" may stay in a landfill for 70 years. A glass bottle will not melt until it reaches a temperature of 2,000° F. Melting glass wastes a lot of energy even if you recycle it! The paper bag you use could have been replaced by a reusable one made of cotton or cloth. This Earth Action will help you to reduce the amount of garbage you send to the landfill.

EARTH ACTION
- Package your food and drink in materials that are designed for more than one use (airtight plastic containers with lids for sandwiches, salads, and snacks, and a thermos for your drink).
- Use your backpack, a reusable bag, or a cloth bag to carry your lunch.

MATERIALS
- Cloth bag or backpack, plastic containers, and a thermos.

TIME
- About 15 minutes to search through cupboards.

RESOURCE SAVINGS
You save landfill space, resources, and energy! This action needs repeating. For committing to a new habit for the Earth, you deserve a pat on the back!

GLOBAL 3 HERO

BAG BAGS

WHY ACT? When you buy things at a store, the person behind the counter often puts it in a bag for you. On just one shopping trip to a mall, you could end up with five or six bags! This Earth Action will help you to reduce the number of bags you use.

RESOURCE SAVINGS

Paper is made out of trees. If you say "no thanks" to two bags a day, that's over 700 bags per year, and you will save one 15-year-old tree from destruction! If you listen carefully to the leaves of a tree rustled by a breeze, you will hear the tree saying, "Thanks!"

EARTH ACTION
• Take your backpack or cloth bag when you go shopping. Whether you need to store your lunch, want to buy a gift for a friend, or just want to keep a sweatshirt handy, your backpack is the answer!
• The next time a store clerk asks, "Paper or plastic?" the answer is, "Neither. I have my own!"

MATERIALS
• One sturdy backpack.

TIME
• No time at all!

GLOBAL HERO 1

WIPE SWIPE

WHY ACT? Paper napkins are popular because they are inexpensive and handy to use. However, they are not cheap for the Earth. Paper napkins use up a lot of trees. While napkins are only a small part of the paper problem, they are a good example of the needless waste of trees. This Earth Action will help you take a step toward reducing your overall paper use.

EARTH ACTION
- Volunteer to set the table for meals this week.
- Swipe the wipes! Set out cloth napkins or small hand towels instead of paper napkins.
- If someone asks, "Why cloth?" just say, "Why waste a tree?"
- Keep a cloth towel handy in the kitchen at all times for mopping up small spills and wiping hands.

MATERIALS
- Cloth napkins or small cotton hand towels.

TIME
- No time at all!

GLOBAL HERO 1

RESOURCE SAVINGS
You save trees and the energy to make paper, and landfill space. While the impact on the Earth seems small, it is a visible change in the way you live.

DIRT

GESUNDHEIT!

WHY ACT? Hay fever, dust, wind, pollen—there are many reasons why people sneeze. When you sneeze, what do you reach for? When you have a runny nose, what do you use? A paper tissue or a handkerchief? By using a handkerchief, you eliminate the need for tissues and the box. This Earth Action, like "Bag Bags" and "Wipe Swipe," will help you to reduce the amount of paper you use unnecessarily.

RESOURCE SAVINGS

You save trees and the energy to make paper tissues.

EARTH ACTION
• Carry a washable handkerchief or colorful bandana in your pocket or backpack. Now you don't have to run for the tissue box when you feel a sneeze coming on!

MATERIALS
• Handkerchief or colorful bandana.

TIME
• Just a few minutes to rummage through a drawer for a handkerchief.

IF YOUR EYES ARE BIGGER THAN YOUR STOMACH

WHY ACT? Do you find that your eyes are sometimes bigger than your stomach? When you order food at a restaurant, do you end up with a "doggie bag"? That packaging has a cost to the Earth, as you have already learned. But what can you do about it? This Earth Action will help you to avoid unnecessary packaging.

EARTH ACTION
- Bring your backpack or cloth bag to the restaurant, along with a clean, durable, reusable plastic container that has a lid.
- When you are finished with your meal, take out your container and put any leftovers in it.
- If the waiter or waitress asks you if you want a doggie bag, just bag your own!
- See if anyone in your family would like you to bring a container for them.

MATERIALS
- A backpack and a durable, reusable container that can be sealed tight.

TIME
- About 15 seconds!

GLOBAL HERO 2

RESOURCE SAVINGS
You save paper, aluminum foil, Styrofoam, and the energy to produce this packaging. For making this action a good habit in your new lifestyle, the Earth is smiling at you!

NO THANKS!

LET IT ROT

COME ON IN!

COMPOST

WHY ACT?

A few scraps of food left on your plate at the end of a meal is garbage, right? Only if you send it to a landfill. Much of our food waste is needlessly sent to landfills when it can actually be composted instead. This Earth Action will show you how to compost your food scraps to turn them back into fresh soil that can grow new plants again.

RESOURCE SAVINGS

You save landfill space. A lot of landfills will go to waste when kids like you start composting!

Would you like to amaze your friends? Bury an egg in the middle of your mound. Compost mounds can reach temperatures of 125° F to 140° F in just a week! That's hot enough to boil an egg. The egg should be hard-boiled in 2 or 3 days. (This is an experiment, so don't eat the egg.)

EARTH ACTION

- Ask your parent(s) for permission to set up a compost pile in the yard. If you live in a city, you can still compost using a worm bucket. Call your local plant nursery for details.
- Set a bucket with a tight-fitting lid next to your kitchen trash can. After every meal, scrape your non-meat leftovers into the bucket and close it tight.
- Every few days or so, take your scrap bucket outside and add the contents to your compost pile.
- A compost mound can be made of food scraps only, or can have yard waste in it as well. Here's how:
  ✓ Put a layer of sticks 3 feet long and 3 feet wide on the ground.
  ✓ Add a 2- or 3-inch layer of dry brown leaves or soil.
  ✓ Add a 2- or 3-inch layer of green grass clippings.
  ✓ Dig a hole in the middle of your mound, and drop in your leftovers, if you have it.
  ✓ Cover the hole with soil or yard waste to discourage animals from having a picnic.
  ✓ Water your compost lightly several afternoons a week.
  ✓ Stir and turn it with a rake or shovel every week or so.
- If you don't have any of the above materials, don't worry. Just about anything that comes from plants will turn back into soil, given time.
- Volunteer to be your family's household composter!

Note: Your family can purchase a composter instead of building one.

MATERIALS
- Food scraps, bucket and lid, sticks, and yard waste.

TIME
- About 1 hour for setup, 3 minutes every few days for care.

GLOBAL HERO 3

EVERY LITTLE BIT HELPS

WHY ACT? Almost no matter where you look nowadays, you see litter. You find cigarette butts, candy wrappers, newspapers, and more littering the landscape of America. Some people throw stuff "away" on city streets, in wildlife parks, and on country roads. The sad part is that people are the only creatures on Earth who litter! Animals can often be hurt by human litter. Birds and fish can strangle in six-pack rings, and animals that eat Styrofoam can die.

You may not personally litter, and it may make you mad to see others do it. But you can do something about it. By doing this Earth Action, you can make your neighborhood safer for animals and more beautiful at the same time.

EARTH ACTION
• Get a few friends together, choose a site, and pick it up!
• If possible, recycle any litter.

MATERIALS
• Gloves for each person in your group, plastic bags or other container to collect the litter, and signs that say "Pitch In" to alert passersby.

TIME
• Plan on several hours!

GLOBAL 3 HERO

RESOURCE SAVINGS

You improve the natural environment. You can be proud of the difference you are making for your world!

ARTIST AT WORK

WHY ACT? How many pounds of paper do you think you use in one year? 100 pounds? 200? Actually, the real number is almost 600 pounds per year! Only about 45 pounds of that goes to recycling centers, while more than 500 pounds goes to landfills.

The key here is to use the other side of the page when doing homework or drawing. This Earth Action will help you to cut paper use in half.

RESOURCE SAVINGS

You save up to 300 pounds of paper per year. That's enough paper to cover the outside of a small skyscraper.

EARTH ACTION
- Label a box "Paper" and keep it in your room or wherever you work.
- Once you use one side of a piece of paper, add it to the box.
- Whenever you feel like doodling or drawing, use paper from the box.
- Cut some up for scrap, and leave it near the phone for messages.

MATERIALS
- Box, marker, and used paper.

TIME
- About 5 minutes.

GLOBAL HERO 1

TRASH OR TREASURE

WHY ACT? The "trash" you have built up over the years can become someone else's "treasure"! If you do a careful search around your home, you will probably find lots of toys, clothes, games, and other things that you no longer have a use for. This Earth Action will help you to find good homes for some of the things you have outgrown or no longer want.

EARTH ACTION
• Round up any items you no longer use.
• Show your parent(s) your collection. They may want to take some of the items that they consider special and store them for you to hand down to your children.
• Recycle the remaining items by trading them with your friends or donating them to a nonprofit agency such as the Goodwill or the Salvation Army.

MATERIALS
• Boxes and bags.

TIME
• About 2 hours for you to round up and sort through your stuff.

GLOBAL
3
HERO

RESOURCE SAVINGS

You save all the resources it would take to make more of what you're giving away!

Box of Old Stuff

BACK BY POPULAR DEMAND

WHY ACT? How much garbage do you produce? Just a couple of pounds a day maybe? That means that in one year, you produce almost 800 pounds of garbage, which ends up in a landfill! That's equal to the weight of one very large gorilla!

Landfill areas are filling up and closing. It is becoming difficult to site new landfills because no one wants them in their community. You can learn to recycle your own garbage. This Earth Action will show you how to create a recycling center in your home for everyone to use.

RESOURCE SAVINGS

You save sending over half your garbage on a permanent trip to the landfill!

EARTH ACTION
- Call or visit your local recycling center to see what is recyclable in your community.
- Place four bags or boxes in some out-of-the-way spot.
- Label the bags or boxes "Glass," "Cans," "Newspaper," and "Plastic."
- Show your family where things go.
- Save, clean, and separate all your recyclables.
- Take off bottle caps and rings, as they are not recyclable in most places.
- If your community does not have a pickup service, take your recyclables to the recycling center.

MATERIALS
- Bags or boxes, markers, and transportation.

TIME
- 30 minutes for setup.

GLOBAL HERO 3

MY RECYCLING CENTER

GLASS   CANS   NEWSPAPER   PLASTIC

RELATING TO NATURE: BRANCHING OUT

WHY ACT? Paper makes up one-third of all landfills. The sad part is that paper is recyclable and need not be in a landfill. Paper is made from trees. The average kid will use seven trees a year to live his or her life. Trees also breathe in carbon dioxide. This prevents it from going into the atmosphere and causing global warming. This five week program will help you to save at least two of those trees. And this Earth Action will help you to appreciate trees so that you will be more aware whenever you do use paper.

EARTH ACTION

- Find a tree that you think is special. Feel the bark. Trace the lines and look for places where insects or animals live. If it's a warm day, lie down in the shade of your tree. What do you see? Breathe in the oxygen this tree is making for you. What do trees give you besides oxygen?
- Draw a picture, or write a poem or short story about your tree.
- Share your creation with someone else, or take someone to your tree.
- Post your creation in your room to remind you of the importance of all trees.

MATERIALS

- Pen, paper (recycled), and markers.

TIME

- About 2 hours.

GLOBAL HERO 1

RESOURCE SAVINGS

If we appreciate trees' special role in improving our lives, reducing global warming, and adding beauty, we will be more careful in how we use them.

JOURNEY NOTES

_____
_____
_____
_____
_____
_____
_____
_____
_____
_____
_____
_____
_____
_____
_____
_____
_____
_____
_____
_____
_____

WASTING WATER IS ALL WET—TRAVEL LOG

Actions	Action Plan		Shown to Parent(s)	Action Done	Points
Am I Clean Yet?	Day:	Time:	☐	☐	3
Go with the Flow	Day:	Time:	☐	☐	2
All Bottled Up	Day:	Time:	☐	☐	2
Tanks A Lot	Day:	Time:	☐	☐	3
Scrub-A-Dub Tub	Day:	Time:	☐	☐	2
Scrub-A-Dub Rub	Day:	Time:	☐	☐	1
Scrub-A-Dub Hub	Day:	Time:	☐	☐	1
AquaCop	Day:	Time:	☐	☐	3
Pearly Whites	Day:	Time:	☐	☐	1
Relating to Nature: Pondering Water	Day:	Time:	☐	☐	1

Points Needed: 10   Global Hero Points Earned ☐

WASTING WATER IS ALL WET

YOUR GUIDE: THE FROG

I am Pondsy, your guide for the second part of your journey, "Wasting Water is All Wet." I know the secrets of water. Did you know that frogs are one of the animals on Earth that can live in two worlds? I live in the water world and in the world of air breathers. I'm a natural connection between people and what is happening below the surface of the water. As your guide for the second part of your journey, I will share all that I know about water.

Why should you be concerned about water? When you turn on the faucet, there seems to be an endless supply of it, right? The truth is, almost all the water that ever was or will be on Earth is on it right now! The water the dinosaurs drank is the same water you drink. In this part of the journey, you will learn how to do your part to make sure there is enough clean water to drink, wash with, and enjoy as you grow up.

AM I CLEAN YET?

WHY ACT? How much water does it take to get you clean? The average shower uses 50 gallons in 10 minutes (5 gallons per minute)! Do you think you could get clean with about half that much water? This Earth Action will help you to be more careful with your personal water use.

EARTH ACTION
- Keep your showers to a 5-minute maximum.
- If you have a shower head with an on/off switch, use it. If not, find out if your local utility company has low-flow shower heads and get one. In many cases, utility companies give them away for free! You can also purchase them in hardware stores.

MATERIALS
- Low-flow shower head, and watch or clock (optional).

TIME
- A few minutes to phone the utility company or purchase your low-flow showerhead.

GLOBAL 3 HERO

RESOURCE SAVINGS

You save at least 9,125 gallons of water a year! That is enough drinking water to last you until your 100th birthday! Your action has saved a lot of drinking water for all the animals on the Earth!

WAIT, THIS DOESN'T FEEL RIGHT...

SOAP

Low Flow

GO WITH THE FLOW

WHY ACT? Every time you flush the average toilet, about 6 gallons of water is used. Even if you have a low-flow toilet, you still probably flush unnecessarily several times a day. That wastes gallons of clean freshwater, which comes out of the same pipes as your drinking water. This water could have been used for showering, cleaning, or making ice cubes! But it ended up going to the toilet tank, as does almost 40 percent of the water that comes to your home. This Earth Action will help you to cut at least half the amount of water you use to flush human waste down the drain.

RESOURCE SAVINGS

By not flushing, if you have a standard toilet, you save 6 gallons each time. You will save somewhere near 3 flushes a day per person, which is 12 flushes a day for a family of four. That's enough water saved in 1 year to fill an Olympic-sized swimming pool.

EARTH ACTION
- Don't flush the toilet if all you did was add a little urine to the water. Go by this rule: "If it's yellow, let it mellow. If it's brown, flush it down."
- There is a catch, though! What if the rest of the family doesn't want to do this? This is one action the rest of the family has to agree to do.

MATERIALS
- Just your family's agreement.

TIME
- No time involved!

GLOBAL HERO 2

STAY MELLOW, MAN

ALL BOTTLED UP

WHY ACT? How much water goes down the drain before you get water cold enough to drink? 1 cup? 2 cups? 6? On average, 24 cups of clean water go down the drain before the water is cold enough to drink!

This is wasteful. If you live in a city or the suburbs, the clean drinking water that goes down the drain has to go to a sewage plant and then to a water treatment plant before it will be clean enough again for humans to drink! This Earth Action will help you to reduce to zero the amount of water you waste at the faucet!

EARTH ACTION
• Fill a pitcher with tap water every morning, and keep it in the refrigerator. Now you have cold, refreshing drinking water on hand at all times.

MATERIALS
• Pitcher and lid or bottle.

TIME
• About 1 minute every morning!

GLOBAL HERO 2

RESOURCE SAVINGS
You save about **550 gallons** of water per person in your home each year. That's enough water for you to take a short shower every day for 3 weeks! Now no one in your home will have to let the tap run.

TANKS A LOT

WHY ACT? Older tanks hold an average of 6 gallons, but new small tanks hold about 1.5 gallons, and that is all that is needed to flush. If you have an older tank, each time you flush, 4.5 extra gallons go down the drain. This Earth Action will help you to reduce the amount of water that fills your older tank so that less is wasted each time you flush.

RESOURCE SAVINGS

A half gallon of water is saved each time anyone flushes the toilet. You save about 1,500 gallons of water in 1 year. That's enough freshwater for a family of four to have daily drinking water for over 4 years!

EARTH ACTION
• Clean an empty half-gallon plastic container. Soak the container to remove labels.
• Fill the container about half full with wet sand or gravel.
• Secure the lid on tightly.
• Have a parent supervise you as you put your homemade "toilet dam" in the corner of the tank. Make sure it does not interfere with any moving parts.

NOTE: If you have a newer, water-saver toilet which only uses a few gallons to flush, you won't need to do this.

MATERIALS
• Half-gallon jug and lid, and sand or gravel.

TIME
• About a half hour.

GLOBAL HERO 3

(22)

SCRUB-A-DUB TUB

WHY ACT? There is a water-efficient way to go about washing small amounts of dishes. Washing a small load in a dishwasher wastes up to 12 gallons of water. Even washing dishes by hand while the rinse water runs is a waste. This Earth Action will help you to reduce your water waste.

EARTH ACTION
- Fill a small tub or large pot with hot, soapy water. Put dishes in and let them soak a bit.
- Scrub dishes with a cotton cloth or sponge.
- Fill another tub or pot about two-thirds full with hot water. Dunk and swish dishes in the rinse water to remove soap film.

MATERIALS
- Two small tubs or large pots, and biodegradable dish liquid soap.

TIME
- About 15 minutes per meal to wash dishes.

GLOBAL 2 HERO

RESOURCE SAVINGS

Washing by hand once a day in this fashion uses about 4 gallons of water instead of up to 12. You could save 8 gallons each day, or almost 3,000 gallons in 1 year. That's enough water saved for 3 years' worth of dishwashing! And if you already wash by hand but leave the water running when you wash, this method will save hundreds more gallons per year. The Earth and your family thank you!

♪ RUB-A-DUB-TUB ♪♫

RINSE TUB

SCRUB-A-DUB RUB

WHY ACT? How many times have you been asked, "Did you wash your hands?" You've probably been asked this at least as many times as you've sat at the kitchen table! If you count washing up in the morning, you probably clean your hands and face about four times each day. That's a lot of germs going down the drain, but the germs aren't the only thing going down. Letting the water run hard for even 30 seconds each time you wash costs the Earth 3 gallons per day! This Earth Action will help you cut your water for cleaning up down to about a gallon a day.

RESOURCE SAVINGS

You save about 2 gallons of water each day. Making this action a habit means that in 3 years you will use the same amount of water as you would have used in 1 year washing the old-fashioned way!

EARTH ACTION
- Run the water at low force to wet your hands and the soap, then turn it off.
- Soap up, then run the water at low force to rinse off.

MATERIALS
- Soap and grime!

TIME
- Only a few seconds longer than usual.

GLOBAL HERO 1

PEOPLE SINK

FROG SINK

SCRUB-A-DUB HUB

WHY ACT? If your family has a car, washing it on a warm afternoon can be more than just a chore. There's nothing like having a little fun while you get a job done for your family. However, the outdoor faucet can be a big source of waste. At 5 gallons a minute running out of the hose, it takes only 20 minutes to use up 100 gallons! This Earth Action will help you to cut this water use down to about 15 gallons.

EARTH ACTION
- Put a nozzle on the hose that allows you to control the flow of water. A no-cost option is to crimp the hose, run to the faucet, and shut the water off.
- Fill a bucket with soap and water to allow your sponges or cotton rags to stay soapy and free of dirt.
- Be mindful of the detergent you use to clean your car. A mild dishwashing liquid will do just as good a job as strong detergents at removing road grime.

MATERIALS
- Hose, nozzle, bucket, sponges or rags, and biodegradable dishwashing liquid.

TIME
- No extra time required.

RESOURCE SAVINGS
You save as much as 85 gallons per wash. That's enough water to wash about six relatives' cars and become a family hero, as well as a Global Hero for doing this action!

GLOBAL HERO 1

OOPS, DON'T FORGET THIS SPOT

AQUACOP

WHY ACT? A small drip from a leaky faucet is just a drop in the bucket, right? Wrong! Even a slow leak can waste 4 to 5 gallons of water each day. If you count up all the possible leak spots in your home, there's a great chance for huge water losses! This Earth Action will help you to sharpen your senses of sight and hearing as you search for leaks.

RESOURCE SAVINGS

If you find any leaks, you save a lot of water! You are now a resource detective for the Earth!

EARTH ACTION
- Scout around your entire home looking for possible leak spots. Try around indoor and outdoor faucets, under toilets, near shower and tub fixtures, and so on.
- Spend a couple of minutes searching for clues at each spot. Look for drips, water stains, mildew. Listen for toilet tanks that continue to run.
- Make a list of the places where you find leaks.
- Report leaks to parent(s), and encourage them to repair trouble spots.

MATERIALS
- Paper, pencil, and keen senses!

TIME
- 30 seconds per faucet.

GLOBAL 3 HERO

PEARLY WHITES

WHY ACT? The average bathroom sink runs about 1 ½ gallons of water down the drain every minute. Letting the water run as you brush you teeth–for 3 minutes in the morning and 3 minutes at night–wastes as much as 9 gallons of water per day. That's over 3,000 gallons each year! This Earth Action will help you to reduce your water use to just a few ounces each time you brush.

EARTH ACTION
- Get a small cup from the kitchen cupboard.
- Put enough water in the cup to wet your brush now and rinse your mouth later.
- Wet your toothbrush, then brush your teeth.
- Rinse your mouth with the water from the cup.
- Add a little more water to the cup to swish your brush clean.
- Wash your cup regularly to remove germs.

MATERIALS
- Cup, toothbrush, toothpaste.

TIME
- About 3 minutes to gather your goods.

RESOURCE SAVINGS
You save over 3,000 gallons of water a year. That's enough water for each person in a family of four to take a 5-minute shower for 6 weeks!

GLOBAL 1 HERO

RELATING TO NATURE: PONDERING WATER

WHY ACT? Water—70 percent of the Earth is covered by it. Most of your body is made up of it. You and I could only live a few days without it. Water can be like people's emotions. It can be warm and gentle, choppy and rough, or cold and angry. Water, as it is in nature, is really a lot like you and me. This Earth Action will help to deepen your appreciation for nature's wet wonder.

RESOURCE SAVINGS

None, but a big kiss from the Earth for noticing.

EARTH ACTION
- Find a natural body of water. It could be a stream, lake, ocean, and so on.
- Relax and watch the water. What color is it? Does it look calm or angry? What else do you notice about the water?
- Draw a picture, or write a poem or short story about your special body of water.
- Share your drawing or writing with a friend.
- Post your drawing or writing in your room to remind you of the value of water.

MATERIALS
- Markers, paper, pen, and water!

TIME
- About a half hour.

GLOBAL HERO 1

JOURNEY NOTES

START

JOURNEY NOTES

_____

_____

_____

_____

_____

_____

_____

_____

_____

_____

_____

_____

_____

_____

_____

_____

_____

GETTING A CHARGE OUT OF SAVING ENERGY—TRAVEL LOG

Actions	Action Plan		Shown to Parent(s)	Action Done	Points
A Bright Idea	Day:	Time:	☐	☐	1
Chill Out in Your Room	Day:	Time:	☐	☐	3
A Fridge Physical	Day:	Time:	☐	☐	3
Better a Sweater	Day:	Time:	☐	☐	3
Charge It!	Day:	Time:	☐	☐	2
Getting There on Your Own Steam	Day:	Time:	☐	☐	2
We All Ride a Yellow Busmarine	Day:	Time:	☐	☐	2
Squash Party	Day:	Time:	☐	☐	2
Shady Friends	Day:	Time:	☐	☐	3
Relating to Nature: An Enlightening Experience	Day:	Time:	☐	☐	1

Points Needed: 12   Global Hero Points Earned ☐

GETTING A CHARGE OUT OF SAVING ENERGY

YOUR GUIDE: THE EAGLE

I am Sky, your guide for the third part of your journey, "Getting a Charge out of Saving Energy." I enjoy a special relationship with the Sun, for I fly so high that I come closer to it than any other creature on Earth. The Sun does not get a lot of visitors, and so we have become close friends. Over the years, the Sun has told me many stories. I would like to share one of those stories with you about where energy comes from.

The Sun has always given energy to plants. Plants eat sunshine in order to get energy and grow! Animals can't eat sunshine, so they eat the bodies of plants and other animals to get the Sun's energy that is stored in them. Millions of years ago, dinosaurs roamed the Earth. Over a long, long period of time, the dinosaurs, other animals, and plants that died were slowly buried in the Earth, but the Sun's energy was stored in them! Inside the Earth, under great heat and pressure, the dinosaurs, plants, and animals turned into fossil fuels (coal, oil, and gas), which are still there today. Humans drill into the Earth to get the fossil fuels.

People want the fossil fuels because the Sun's energy that was stored in the creatures that lived millions of years ago is still there! These fossil fuels are used in your home so that you can listen to your MP3 or CD player, stay warm, read by electric lights, and watch TV. They are also burned in cars, buses, and other kinds of transportation so that you can get to school quickly, visit relatives or just go to the mall. Isn't it amazing that the energy of dinosaurs and ancient plants has such an effect on your life?

However, there are two problems that concern scientists about fossil fuels. First, since this fuel comes from ancient plants and animals, when will the supply run out? It takes the Earth millions of years to make fossils. At the rate humans are using them up, this energy source can't last much longer.

The second problem is that when these fossil fuels are burned, they give off gases. You have probably seen or smelled the gases behind cars and buses, or seen them drifting from chimneys on cold mornings. The gases are bad for the air you and I breathe. Even though it gets washed from the sky by rain, it hurts fish and your drinking water, and it harms the forests. Scientists tell us the carbon dioxide gases trap the Earth's heat, causing it to warm up too much. This is known as global warming. Global warming is causing many problems including severe hurricanes, droughts and flooding.

How you use energy affects not only your family and you, but also every other living thing on Earth. As your guide, I will teach you how to use energy with greater care and wisdom.

A BRIGHT IDEA

WHY ACT?

As you know, we have to be wise in how we use our energy. Burning fossil fuels causes pollution and global warming. Even if your home electricity supply doesn't come from fossil fuels, you'll still save money. Instead of going to waste, those dollars could be used for many other things, such as your allowance. By taking this Earth Action, you will save money, improve the quality of the air, and save energy.

EARTH ACTION
• If you are the last one out of a room, turn off the lights. It does not cost any more money to turn them back on a few minutes later if you need them again.
• Turn off the TV when not in use.
• Turn off the radio or CD player when you leave the room.

MATERIALS
• A keen pair of eyes!

TIME
• A couple of extra seconds.

GLOBAL HERO 1

DON'T FORGET THE LIGHT.

RESOURCE SAVINGS
You save wasted energy, your parents' money, and if your home uses fossil fuels, you save air pollution and reduce global warming! Think of all the energy you can save in your lifetime!

CHILL OUT IN YOUR ROOM

WHY ACT? Air leaks are a major way that energy is lost from your home. Leaks around doors and windows allow warm air out and cold air in. This causes your home heating system to work longer and harder—another big energy waste! This Earth Action will help you to have a toasty room and be a good example for the rest of your home.

EARTH ACTION
- See if your room needs cold weather insulation by doing a cold air test. Feel around windows and the edges of wall outlets for leaks.
- If you discover even a small breeze around your windows, then they need to be weatherstripped. If you feel cold air coming out the edges of your wall outlets, then they need to have outlet insulators.
- Report your findings to your parent(s). Ask your parent(s) to take you to a hardware store to buy weatherstripping and insulators. These should only cost a few dollars and will save your parent(s) money within the year and every year after that!
- Have your parent(s) follow the directions on the packages.
- Now that you know how to do the cold air test, volunteer to be a guide for any members of your family who would like to weatherize another room.

MATERIALS
- Weatherstripping, insulators, screwdriver, and your parent(s).

TIME
- Plan on a couple of hours to test, travel, and tuck!

GLOBAL HERO 3

RESOURCE SAVINGS

You save for your family some of the money spent on energy, and you save for everyone the air pollution and global warming caused by burning fossil fuels.

WEATHER STRIPPING

A FRIDGE PHYSICAL

WHY ACT? What is chilly, bigger than a breadbox, and opened 32,000 times a year by a family of four? Your refrigerator! You alone open a fridge about 8,000 times a year! Did you know that it takes a lot of energy to run a fridge? The fridge is the biggest energy appliance in your home. It uses as much energy as a washer and dryer, dishwasher, and CD player in one day!

The energy for your home probably comes from a utility company that burns fossil fuels. The more energy you need to keep food cool, the more you pollute and contribute to global warming. This Earth Action will help your refrigerator to run more efficiently, and help you to cut back the number of times you need to open the door.

RESOURCE SAVINGS

You save energy, money, air pollution and reduce global warming caused by burning fossil fuels.

EARTH ACTION
- Test the tightness of the seal on your fridge door. Open the door, slide a piece of paper between the door seal and the fridge, then close the door. If the paper pulls out easily, recommend a new seal to your parent(s).
- Have your parent(s) vacuum the coils. Wipe the coils to remove dust. Cleaning the coils helps them to take heat from the fridge much better. The coils are usually on the back side or behind a grate on the bottom. Watch out! The coils can get hot!
- If you have a thermometer, place it in the fridge; it should be around 38°F, while the freezer should be around 5°F. If it's higher or lower, ask your parent(s) to adjust the thermostat.
- Now pledge to open the door less and keep it open for a shorter time when you do open it.

MATERIALS
- Paper, vacuum cleaner, rag and thermometer (optional).

TIME
- About 15 minutes every few months.

GLOBAL **3** HERO

DIDN'T YOU JUST OPEN ME?

BETTER A SWEATER

WHY ACT? In most homes, the thermostat is set a little warmer than it needs to be. This wastes energy, and money, and causes air pollution and global warming. Most families don't know that they can turn the thermostat down a little and still be comfortable. A small change in the thermostat will make a noticeable difference, since home heating accounts for more than 25% of your parent(s)' energy bill. This Earth Action offers you the chance to save energy and be an Earth guide by sharing what you've learned with your family.

RESOURCE SAVINGS

You save energy and money. If your home uses fossil fuels, you save air pollution and reduce global warming. The trees thank your family and you for letting them breathe more easily.

EARTH ACTION
- Call a family meeting. Share this action with your family. Ask if they would like to do this with you. If your family agrees, take turns setting the thermostat.
- During the days, set thermostat at "sweater" temperature—somewhere between 65°F to 68°F.
- Before you go to bed at night, turn the thermostat down to "blanket" temperature—between 55°F and 58°F.

MATERIALS
- Sweater or sweatshirt.

TIME
- A few minutes for the meeting, a few seconds to set the thermostat.

CHARGE IT!

WHY ACT? While battery-operated toys may be fun, they are costly to keep powered. Buying batteries for the life of your toy is expensive. It's also expensive for the Earth! "Disposable" batteries contain toxics that can seep out into landfills and pollute your drinking water! Kids who have a lot of battery operated toys, throw away lots of batteries each year. Switching from non-rechargeable batteries to chargeables will greatly reduce the amount of batteries going to landfills, helping you save money and the Earth.

EARTH ACTION

- Do a count of your battery-operated toys. See which ones use the same size batteries. Figure out the least number of rechargeable batteries you would need to buy. Remember, it's difficult to use more than one toy at a time anyway.
- Ask you parent(s) to consider buying rechargeable batteries and a charger for your toys as well as for their battery-operated things. While they will spend more money to get started with rechargeables, each one of these batteries lasts as long as 25 regular batteries! Using a charger will pay for itself in just a few months.
- Charge your batteries only when you need them. Most rechargeable batteries can be charged 100 times!

MATERIALS

- A battery charger and rechargeable batteries.

TIME

- About 3 hours to charge your batteries. Plan ahead for the sake of the Earth.

RESOURCE SAVINGS

You save the Earth from pollution caused by battery chemicals such as mercury, lead, sulfuric acid, and zinc. You also save money, landfill space, and drinking water.

GLOBAL HERO 2

GETTING THERE ON YOUR OWN STEAM

WHY ACT? If you live in a place where there is no easy access to public transportation, you have to depend on your parent(s) every time you want to go somewhere. This Earth Action gives you a chance to do something a lot of kids today don't easily do—actually wear out a pair of sneakers! You will be able to set your own schedule, reduce air pollution, and if you go with a friend, catch up on the latest news.

RESOURCE SAVINGS

You save for your parent(s) money, time, and wear and tear on the family vehicle. By not burning fossil fuels, you make the air cleaner for birds, trees, fish, and all living creatures and reduce global warming .

EARTH ACTION
- Look for places to walk or ride your bike instead of asking your parent(s) to take you.
- Check with your parent(s) to make sure the route you plan to take is safe.
- Choose at least one place this week to walk to, then look for more opportunities every week thereafter.
- See if a friend wants to go. It makes walking more fun!

MATERIALS
- Whatever means of self transportation you want: walk, run, bike, roller-blade, or skateboard.

TIME
- Not long to a healthier, cleaner life and planet.

GLOBAL HERO 2

WE ALL RIDE IN A YELLOW BUSMARINE

WHY ACT? Here is another opportunity to cut down on the amount of air pollution and global warming you create. Opportunities for talking with friends or catching up on homework make this a winning action for you. It will also please your parent(s). Instead of asking your parent(s) for a ride to school, take the school bus. In most communities, bus stops are not too hard to reach and the buses are usually on time. Remember, the bus goes by whether you're on it or not!

EARTH ACTION
- Find out when and where to catch the school bus.
- Ride the "yellow busmarine" from now on!

MATERIALS
- School bus schedule.

TIME
- Just a few minutes extra.

GLOBAL HERO 2

RESOURCE SAVINGS

Being the cause of less air pollution means that you're making the air cleaner for eagles and other flying friends. And you are reducing global warming for the whole planet.

YELLOW BUSMARINE

SQUASH PARTY

WHY ACT? Many places to which you travel probably have other kids your age traveling there, too. If fewer vehicles were used to get kids from one place to another, think of the fossil fuels, clean air, road use, and time that would be saved! This is also a great opportunity for you to "show off" your new friends to your parent(s). If you don't know many kids where you're going, this Earth Action is a great way to make new friends while you reduce air pollution and global warming.

RESOURCE SAVINGS

You reduce car mileage, gas money, air pollution, and road use. You make your parent(s) happy because they have more time to do other things. You also reduce global warming.

EARTH ACTION
- When you are at the next activity where you meet other kids, find out who lives near you and swap phone numbers.
- Give the phone numbers to your parent(s) so that they can set up a car pool.
- Think of all the places you go to where you can have a "squash party" to get there.

MATERIALS
- New or old friends, and a car.

TIME
- When it's your parent(s)' turn to drive, just a few extra minutes to pick up and drop off friends.

GLOBAL HERO 2

OOF!

SHADY FRIENDS

WHY ACT? Trees provide shade to keep you cool. In winter, they shed their leaves, letting the Sun's warm rays through. Trees hold the soil in place. They absorb carbon dioxide, which causes global warming, and make oxygen for you to breathe. They are natural homes for many of the Earth's animals. Trees add beauty and color to your world. This Earth Action will show you how trees can help cool your house in the summer, possibly saving your parent(s) money on air conditioning.

EARTH ACTION
- If you live in a house with a yard, ask your parent(s) if they would like a tree planted to provide more shade or add beauty to the yard.
- Look in the yellow pages for a local tree farm or a tree and shrub nursery.
- Go there with your parent(s) and pick out the special tree you want to plant.
- Another option, if they don't want to spend the money, is to call a local environmental group and ask them if they know where you can get a tree seedling at little or no cost.
- Ask your parent(s) to help you plant your tree on the south side of your home. Follow the planting directions that come with it.
- You could also encourage your parent(s) this year to get a live Christmas tree from your local nursery or tree farm. You can plant it in the spring and watch it grow as you yourself grow!

MATERIALS
- Seedling or tree, shovel, and a planting site.

TIME
- A few minutes to call around and locate a tree, a couple of hours to get it and plant it.

GLOBAL HERO 3

RESOURCE SAVINGS
Once your tree grows large enough to provide shade, it will help keep your home cooler in the summer. This will save your parent(s) money on their cooling bill. You save energy costs for cooling your house. Also, a precious tree is now in your life!

UM, EXCUSE ME

RELATING TO NATURE: AN ENLIGHTENING EXPERIENCE

WHY ACT? The Sun is the source of all energy. It lights your way, keeps you warm, and gives energy to the plants you eat. A calm, quiet feeling comes over people as they watch brilliant sunsets. However, most kids miss a chance to see one of the most awesome creations of nature. This experience has some of the most brilliant colors you'll ever see, and it's Free! Do you know what it could be? You guessed it! A sunrise! This Earth Action will help you to appreciate our Sun, the source of all energy on Earth.

RESOURCE SAVINGS

None. But the Sun is beaming down on you, happy that you've taken the time to appreciate it.

EARTH ACTION
- Check the newspaper to see what time the Sun rises. Make sure you get plenty of sleep the night before.
- If you can, find an open area where you will be able to see the Sun as it breaks over the horizon.
  <u>WARNING: Do not look directly into the Sun!</u>
- Draw or paint a picture of your sunrise. Watercolors and pastels will allow you to capture the brilliant blends of color.
- Write a story about what the Sun will do that day, or write a poem about how it felt to see the sunrise.
- Share your creation with a friend or family member.
- Post your creation in your room to remind you of the precious gifts of the Sun—light, heat, and energy.

MATERIALS
- Newspaper, open area, art supplies, paper, and pen.

TIME
- About a half hour.

GLOBAL HERO 1

START

JOURNEY NOTES

JOURNEY NOTES

GOOD BUYS ARE FOREVER—TRAVEL LOG

Actions	Action Plan		Shown to Parent(s)	Action Done	Points
			☐	☐	1
What Goes Around Came Around	Day:	Time:	☐	☐	3
Toxic Sleuth	Day:	Time:	☐	☐	1
Leave Me a Loan	Day:	Time:	☐	☐	3
Chew On This For Awhile	Day:	Time:	☐	☐	1
Bulk Up	Day:	Time:	☐	☐	2
When the "Gotta Have Its" Attack, Head for the Hills	Day:	Time:	☐	☐	3
Vote for the Earth	Day:	Time:	☐	☐	2
Vegetable Soup	Day:	Time:	☐	☐	3
It Will Grow On You	Day:	Time:	☐	☐	1
Relating to Nature: Second Chances	Day:	Time:			

Points Needed: 11 Global Hero Points Earned ☐

EARTH-FRIENDLY FOREST STORE

HI, I'M MUNK! I CAN SHOW YOU HOW TO SHOP FOR THE EARTH!

HERBS

NUTS

BERRIES

GOOD BUYS ARE FOREVER

YOUR GUIDE: THE CHIPMUNK

I am Munk, your guide for the fourth part of your journey, "Good Buys Are Forever." You may have seen me scurrying about. I'm busy carefully checking out everything I come across, so I rarely have a chance to stop and chat. Because I'm such a good Earth shopper, I was asked to share my knowledge with you about how to shop wisely.

You might think a chipmunk makes for a strange guide, so little and shy. But, really, I have to be a careful shopper, for my Earth home is small and packed with leaves and nuts. I produce almost no waste, never need a bag (I use my cheeks), only choose quality items that will last a long time, and use every part of the items I bring home. Why, just the other day, I made bowls out of acorn caps and a washtub out of half a walnut shell! I get great value out of all the resources I use. The knowledge I will share will help you to do the same. I don't even like to waste time, so let's go!

WHAT GOES AROUND CAME AROUND

WHY ACT? If you're recycling your paper, there is a good chance that within the next year, someone will buy this year's homework and use that paper to draw, write or paint on. While recycling paper is a good step to take, it's only half of the answer. The other half is to buy recycled paper products. This Earth Action will remind you to be on the lookout for these products.

EARTH ACTION
- The next time you need to purchase paper products—notebook paper, special occasion cards (Christmas, Hanukkah, Mother's Day, Valentines Day, etc.), assignment pads, sketch pads, and so on—make sure you look for the recycle symbol. ♻
- If possible, look for paper that is labeled "post-consumer waste"—that's the stuff people like you actually recycled, not just the trimmings from the paper mill floor.

MATERIALS
- Recycled paper products.

TIME
- Just a couple extra seconds to look for the recycle symbol and read labels.

GLOBAL HERO 1

RESOURCE SAVINGS

You save new trees and the extra energy to make paper from scratch. You also get a leafy hug for taking this action.

TOXIC SLEUTH

WHY ACT?

If you look under the sink, in the kitchen closet and in the workroom, shed, or garage, you will probably see a large number of products used to spruce up around the home. The major ones are: 1) cleaning detergents for appliances, floors, clothes, windows, and furniture 2) paints, varnishes, and stains for inside and outside your home and 3) bug repellents, car and yard products. These products will help get the job done, however, many of them contain ingredients that can be harmful to the Earth and, in some cases, you, too.

CONTAINS TOXIC INGREDIENTS... WE BETTER WRITE THIS ONE UP

You and your family need to use these products with care. When products that contain toxics are sprayed, they may harm the air and you. Toxic containing products that are spread on the ground can harm the soil, and the toxics can seep into underground streams and find their way into your drinking water. By taking this Earth Action, you can identify these products that can cause harm and alert your parents to the fact that many of these products have nontoxic alternatives.

RESOURCE SAVINGS

You improve the quality of the air you breathe, the water you drink, and the soil around your neighborhood!

EARTH ACTION

- There are three parts to this Earth Action: (1) make a list of products in your home that might be toxic; (2) find out where to get nontoxic products that will do the same things; and (3) find out how to get rid of all the toxic stuff safely.
- With a parent, do a detective search in all the places in your home where these products may be found. If you don't see advertising on the label that describes the ingredients as Earth-friendly, there's a chance the product contains toxics. WARNING: Do not open any containers. Wash your hands when you are finished.
- Make a list of the possibly toxic products you find (bleach, bug sprays, oven cleaner, paints etc.). Show your parent(s) your list when you are done.
- Call your local hardware store, supermarket, or health food store to see whether they have Earth-friendly products with which you could replace these toxic products. If they do, alert your parent(s) as to where they can find these products. If your local stores do not stock Earth-friendly products, ask them to carry them.
- Use up what you have or call your town or city hall and find out where to properly dispose of toxic stuff.

MATERIALS

- Pencil, paper, and telephone.

TIME

- About 2 or 3 hours.

GLOBAL HERO 3

LEAVE ME A LOAN

WHY ACT? Have you ever thought that your friends have cool stuff? Guess what. . . they probably think you do, too. This Earth Action will show you how you can have cool stuff like theirs without using any more of the Earth's resources or spending any money.

EARTH ACTION
• Become a loaner. Loan something of yours to a friend, who loans you something in exchange. Be clear about how long the loan is for. Be just as responsible with their things as you want them to be with yours.

MATERIALS
• Something worth loaning, something worth borrowing.

TIME
• Just a few minutes to arrange the loan swap!

GLOBAL HERO 1

RESOURCE SAVINGS
You not only save money, since you did not have to purchase the new item, but you also have something new to enjoy at no extra cost to the Earth.

HEY! YOU CAN'T LOAN ME!

CHEW ON THIS FOR AWHILE

WHY ACT?

The single most important action you can take for the Earth is to eat less meat. "Why?" you ask. The water, energy, and land necessary to produce meat uses more of the Earth's resources than almost anything else that you will ever consume and is one of the most significant ways we each contribute to global warming! While beef, chicken, and pork can be raised in ways that carefully use the Earth's resources, chances are the meat in your supermarket demanded a huge amount of chemical fertilizers and pesticides, energy, and water. The beef in your hamburger may well have come from cattle that grazed where the rainforest was cut down so that beef could be raised. This Earth Action will offer you alternative ideas for meals that use less of the Earth's resources.

RESOURCE SAVINGS

For each pound of beef you substitute with vegetables and grains, you save about 2,000 gallons of water! You lessen the reason for the rainforests to be cut down, and you allow more homes for wildlife. You also reduce your impact on global warming. What's more, you save your family money, since meat is so expensive.

EARTH ACTION

The Earth Action this week is to eat two fewer meat meals than usual and to commit to keep looking for ways to eat less meat after this week is over. Here is how to do this:

- Look through cookbooks for tasty nonmeat recipes, then tell your parent(s).
- Ask your parent(s) to make nonmeat meals each week.
- Help prepare these meals.

MATERIALS

- Vegetables, grains, fruits, nuts, and a vegetarian cookbook.

TIME

- A half hour to look through cookbooks and educate yourself; a few minutes to talk with your parent(s) about the food you would like to eat; some time to help prepare meals if that's what your parent(s) and you agree to do.

GLOBAL 3 HERO

TODAY'S MENU
ACORN SOUP
ACORN SALAD
ACORN MUSH
ACORN AND GRAVY
ACORN (PLAIN)

I LOVE THIS PLACE!

BULK UP

WHY ACT? Since you already know about no garbage lunches (from part 1), it is time to buy food that produces less packaging waste. You probably like to have snacks during the day, whether at home or school. The problem is that a lot of snacks come in individually wrapped packages. This packaging adds a good deal of bulk to the waste stream. This Earth Action will further help you to reduce what you send to the landfill.

EARTH ACTION
- When a parent goes to the supermarket this week, ask if you can go so that you can take this action.
- Take along reusable containers or recycled bags to hold bulk purchases and a backpack or cloth bag to carry food home in.
- Once there, search for food that is in bulk packaging: cereal in large boxes, snack packages that are not individually wrapped, and beverages in 2 liter bottles.
- Once you and your family become bulk buyers, you will need to shop less often and you'll also save money.

MATERIALS
- reusable containers, recycled bags, cloth bag or backpack.

TIME
- Less than 1 hour for the trip to and from the supermarket.

RESOURCE SAVINGS

The packaging that doesn't come to your home allows you to reduce the amount of plastic, paper, cellophane, and other wrappings that you would usually send to the landfill. Since packaging costs money, you also will help your parent(s) to save money.

GLOBAL 1 HERO

FRUIT SNACKS GIANT PACKAGE

All Natural Soda Big, Huge Size

THIS WILL LAST A WHILE!

WHEN THE "GOTTA HAVE ITS" ATTACK, HEAD FOR THE HILLS

WHY ACT? Have you ever asked your parent(s) to buy you something, then turned around a few weeks later and wondered why you ever thought that the item was necessary? That happens to a lot of adults, not just kids. People sometimes buy things just to make themselves feel good or just to have something new and different. Also, TV makes things look pretty appealing. It makes you want the stuff advertised. This Earth Action will give you a healthy, free, and fun alternative to spur-of-the-moment shopping.

RESOURCE SAVINGS

Because you did not buy the product you were thinking of, an identical one does not need to take its place on the shelf in the store. Therefore, you reduce the demand for all the materials that the product is made of, the packaging it comes in, the fossil fuels burned to deliver it, and the global warming it produces! You are also doing something good for yourself.

EARTH ACTION
- Instead of buying something to make you feel good, take a hike in nature with a friend, go for a bike ride, or play a game.
- Choose a fun place. Ask your parent(s) to help you make sure your route is safe.

MATERIALS
- A fun, safe route; a no garbage lunch; comfortable shoes and clothing; and transportation.

TIME
- An afternoon or a few hours on the weekend.

GLOBAL HERO 2

- NATURE
- FRIENDS
- FUN
- ADVENTURE

- STUFF TO BUY

VOTE FOR THE EARTH

WHY ACT?

To live our lives, we need to consume things. Everything people use is made from resources that come from the Earth. Buying is fine, but how we choose what to buy is important. When you look at a product, do you think of the two costs it has? There is both the cost in money and the cost to the Earth. Most shoppers think in dollars and not "sense." This Earth Action will help you to buy in a manner that causes the least cost to the Earth.

EARTH ACTION

- Follow the "terrific trio" of guidelines—QPE—when shopping.
  - ✔ Q (quality): Choose products with the best quality, because they last longer.
  - ✔ P (packaging): Examine the packaging. Did the manufacturer use as little as possible, or is there excess packaging? Is the packaging made from recyclable materials?
  - ✔ E (Earth-friendliness): Consider the cost to the Earth. Is the product made from recycled materials? Can it be recycled? Is it locally made? Is it nontoxic? Is it biodegradable?
- Very few things you buy will meet all the terrific trio guidelines. But if you buy with these in mind and find products with one or two, you're on the right path.
- Look for addresses on the labels of the products you normally buy. Write to those companies that need to make changes based on the "terrific trio" guidelines. Ask them to consider more Earth-friendly ways of making or packaging their product so that you can continue to purchase their products. Be specific with your suggestions. Companies really do pay attention. Also, write to companies that have made changes or have made products with the "terrific trio" in mind and let them know that you appreciate what they are doing for the Earth. By voting for the Earth, you send a message to manufacturers to become more Earth-friendly in how they produce and package products. Make voting for the Earth a regular part of your new lifestyle.

MATERIALS

- Money, the terrific trio (QPE), and a keen eye.

TIME

- Just an extra couple seconds looking over each item before you purchase it, and some time to write a few letters.

GLOBAL HERO 3

The EARTH-FRIENDLY Corner

NON-TOXIC AND BIODEGRADABLE

RESOURCE SAVINGS

You save trees, landfill space, air pollution, gasoline, global warming, and more!

VEGETABLE SOUP

WHY ACT? Fresh food from the supermarket tastes great! Eating a nice green salad is a great choice for the Earth and you, isn't it? But each piece of farm-fresh food has a cost to the Earth and you. Much of the produce has been sprayed with harmful pesticides to keep away the bugs. Some produce contains dyes to give it more color, and a wax coating to make it last longer at the market.

There is a solution—organic produce! Organic means that the plant was grown without harmful pesticides. Organically grown food tastes better and is healthier for you and the Earth. It may cost more money to buy, but you can offset that cost with money saved from eating less meat and other resource saving actions. This Earth Action will help you to vote for the Earth and your family—and enjoy tastier salads and vegetable dishes.

EARTH ACTION
- Locate, by phone, a place that sells organic vegetables and fruit. This may be a special section in your local supermarket, a nearby farm stand, or a health food store.
- Ask your family to take you there, then make your selections.
- See whether anyone in your family would like to try some.
- Eat and enjoy!

MATERIALS
- A phone, transportation, money, fresh food, and a healthy appetite!

TIME
- Just a few minutes looking through the yellow pages and talking on the phone, and the travel time to get to the store.

GLOBAL HERO 2

RESOURCE SAVINGS

You save fresh drinking water from being contaminated by toxic pesticides that leach into the soil. Your vote for organic produce will support farmers who grow food this way.

ORGANIC PRODUCE

NO CHEMICALS
NO PESTICIDES

IT WILL GROW ON YOU

WHY ACT? As you may know, the fruits and vegetables that your family buys at the supermarket may be sprayed with several different kinds of pesticides. That produce also had to be shipped to the store from a farm. That means fossil fuels were probably burned, creating air pollution and global warming. Much of the produce has to be kept cool, requiring that more energy is used and more fossil fuels are burned. Also, packaging was needed for shipping and was then discarded or recycled. As you can see, everything humans use has a price tag to the Earth. This Earth Action will offer you an alternative that is fun to do and fascinating to watch.

EARTH ACTION
- Grow your own garden!
- Make a list of your favorite produce and maybe even a few herbs and spices. Find seed packages at your local supermarket, health food store, or local nursery.
- Check the back of each package to see whether the item will grow well in your part of the country.
- Follow the directions for soil preparation, planting, and care.

MATERIALS
- Seeds, compost—if you have it—to put between the rows (not directly on your plants), and a green thumb!

TIME
- A nice spring day and several hours.

GLOBAL HERO 3

RESOURCE SAVINGS You save soil, water, and air from further harm. The Earth will enjoy working with you!

RELATING TO NATURE: SECOND CHANCES

WHY ACT? The half-gallon jug sits in your recycling bin. The toilet paper tube is in another bin. The cardboard box has been broken down to be sent for recycling. You are done with the tin can, and being Earth-wise, you know it is time to recycle it, right? Why not give these items a new life rather than recycle them? This Earth Action helps you to turn recyclables into bird feeders and homes for animals.

EARTH ACTION

- Make a bird feeder out of an empty half-gallon jug. Have an adult poke a hole on both sides near the bottom. Push a stick in one side and out the other. This is for the birds to land on while eating. Next, have an adult cut a hole approximately 1" long by 1/2" high above the stick. Tie a string to the top of the jug, fill with seeds and hang from a tree. Then enjoy watching the birds.
- Give your toilet paper tubes to someone who owns a hamster, gerbil, or the like. Small rodents will climb through them and chew them up to make a nest.
- Make an animal home out of a milk or cleaning product jug. Clean the jug well and soak the labels off. Cut a doorway in one side. Put in notches of trees around your yard. See who moves in.
- Use the cardboard box and tin can to make similar constructions, or come up with new inventions. Make sure tin cans do not have sharp edges or burrs.
- Every once in awhile, replace your constructions with new ones. Recycle the old stuff. Maybe you can keep a log or make sketches of all the different kinds of animals that visit your feeders or homes.

MATERIALS
- Packaging that would otherwise go into recycling bins.

TIME
- A few fun minutes inventing animal homes and toys; hours of fun observing.

RESOURCE SAVINGS

None. But the Earth will appreciate your making resources go a long way.

JOURNEY NOTES

JOURNEY NOTES

_____

_____

_____

_____

_____

_____

_____

_____

_____

_____

_____

_____

_____

_____

_____

_____

_____

_____

WATCH OUT PLANET, HERE I COME!

YOUR GUIDE: THE DOLPHIN

I am Magic, your guide for the fifth and final part of your journey, "Watch Out Planet, Here I Come!" Did you know that we dolphins have a special ability to communicate with each other? The knowledge that I will share with you is how to communicate with someone. This is so obvious that humans often miss it. Humans communicate all the time, right? Well, let's say they talk. When you communicate, someone else has to be listening. Then, you become the listener while they share their ideas in turn. So listen carefully, because I have a special secret to share with you.

There is another guide, one who is more knowledgeable than all the others, including me! Would you like to meet this new guide right now? Just set this book down, go over to a mirror, and see who it is. Did you recognize the newest guide for the Earth? It is you! Think about it for a moment. You have practiced and learned the secrets of the earthworm, the frog, the eagle, and the chipmunk. Now you are gaining my secrets as well. Since you speak the human language, that makes you the perfect guide for the planet! It is time for you to tell others what you have learned from your actions and help them on their journey for the planet.

One more secret: the journey that you have been on will last your whole lifetime. On behalf of all the animals, I thank you for caring!

FRIENDS FOR LIFE

WHY ACT? How hard would you have to work to save twice the Earth's resources you saved on your journey? Twice as hard? Maybe not! Do you know that it's as easy as getting a friend to begin his or her own journey? How hard would you have to work to save three, four, or five times as many resources? This Earth Action will help you to save as many resources as you have friends!

EARTH ACTION

• Your Earth Action is to tell your friends about *Journey for the Planet* to see whether they are interested in going on this adventure, and if they are, to help them get the book.

• If you got your book from a place in your community or book store, go there with your friends.

• If you got your book online, invite your friends to ask their parents to get a copy at www.empowermentinstitute.net. Click on the button that says "Purchase Books."

• Tell your friends that they can count on you to help them on their journey for the planet.

• If they are not interested, just continue to be a good example. Watching you live an environmentally sustainable lifestyle may inspire them to participate in the future.

MATERIALS

• Friends; computer or transportation to the place to get the book; money.

TIME

• A few minutes to talk to your friends and help them get a book.

GLOBAL 3 HERO

SAVE THE PLANET

EARTH-FRIENDLY ZONE

JOURNEY FOR THE PLANET

RESOURCE SAVINGS

Each person you help to start on his or her journey will have similar savings to yours! Isn't that an easy way to double or triple your savings for the Earth?

A COOL SCHOOL

WHY ACT? Look at the new Earth-friendly lifestyle you now enjoy. You practice sustainable living for the Earth and for yourself at home, in restaurants, and in stores. There is one more important place in your life that should be considered: school! Most schools will not be as Earth-friendly as you are, so it may be hard for you to practice your actions there, unless . . . you help to make your school Earth-friendly! This Earth Action will help you set up a plan to make your school cool for the Earth.

EARTH ACTION
- Look back over the Earth-friendly actions you've taken in your home, and see which ones you'd like to also take at school so that you can live your Earth-friendly life there as well. Think about no-garbage lunches, paper recycling, composting, and so on.
- Choose one action that you'd like your school to do.
- Ask to meet with the principal to share your idea.
- Tell your principal that you've already taken this action in your own life, and explain why this action is important for the Earth. Let your principal know that you are willing to help to get it started but that his or her support will be needed as well. Remember also to be a good listener.

MATERIALS
- A clear idea of what you'd like to see happen, your book, and a positive principal.

TIME
- An hour or so to plan your meeting with the principal.

GLOBAL HERO 3

RESOURCE SAVINGS

Whatever your savings were for this action, picture hundreds of other kids having similar savings at school. Think how much CO_2 your school can prevent from causing global warming. That's powerful!

SAVING THE PLANET BEGINS WITH YOU... HIT IT MAGIC!

PUT YOUR FAMILY ON A LOW CARBON DIET

WHY ACT? You have done a lot for the Earth throughout your journey; you must feel great by now! You probably noticed along the way that your parent(s) decide how many of the resources are used in your home. You may have wondered, "How could I help my parents make some of the changes that I have made?" Your parent(s) may also have wondered the same thing, perhaps wishing there was a program for them. This Earth Action will show you how to help your parent(s) live a more Earth-friendly life.

EARTH ACTION
- Ask your parent(s) if they would like to take a journey like yours made for adults. If they say yes, tell them that there is also a program for adults to help them reduce their impact on global warming. It's called *Low Carbon Diet: A 30 Day Program to Lose 5000 Pounds*. They can find out more information about it by visiting www.empowermentinstitute.net/lcd.
- If your parent(s) say no, just continue to be a good example for them. They may change their mind sometime in the future.

MATERIALS
- Computer and your Earth-friendly life.

TIME
- Just a few minutes to speak to your parent(s).

RESOURCE SAVINGS
Your household can save at least 5000 pounds of carbon dioxide which contributes to global warming.

GLOBAL 3 HERO

HI MOM AND DAD, MEET MY NEW FRIEND, MAGIC!

HEROHOOD

WHY ACT? As you went on your journey, you may have found actions you couldn't take because there wasn't support for it in your community. Maybe you couldn't recycle certain items, or maybe you couldn't use your bike to go certain places because there were no bike lanes for safety. Now it is time to see whether you can help your community take on an action that will help you and others live a more Earth-friendly life.

RESOURCE SAVINGS

Resource savings are made for the whole community. You are a local and global hero!

EARTH ACTION
- Go through your book and choose one action that you couldn't take because something you needed wasn't available in your community.
- Think of some ideas for what you would like to see happen in your community so that you could take action.
- Call the mayor's or town supervisor's office and ask for an appointment to share your concerns and ideas. If you have friends who share your concerns and ideas, invite them to come with you.
- Volunteer your time to help the mayor or town supervisor make your ideas happen in your community. For example, volunteer to go to meetings with the mayor or town supervisor and explain to people why you feel this action is important.

MATERIALS
- Friends, your book, ideas about what you would like to see happen, and a positive mayor or town supervisor.

TIME
- An hour or so to plan your meeting.

GLOBAL HERO 3

THANK YOU FOR MAKING THIS COMMUNITY EARTH FRIENDLY!

GLOBAL HERO

A COOL COMMUNITY

 WHY ACT? If many people in your community participate in the *Low Carbon Diet* program, or something similar, your town or city could cut back on its use of fossil fuels which cause global warming. This Earth Action will help you to teach your community to vote for the Earth.

EARTH ACTION
- Ask your mayor or town supervisor to consider starting a Cool Community campaign. The purpose of this campaign is to get as many adults and kids in the community as possible to reduce their emissions of CO_2. For more information on how your community can start a campaign, visit www.empowermentinstitute.net/lcd.
- When you download the information, call the mayor's or town supervisor's office to set up an appointment.
- Bring the materials to share with the mayor or town supervisor.
- If your mayor or town supervisor is interested, offer to help him or her explain the importance of this campaign to your future and that of other kids. Volunteer to go with the mayor or town supervisor to community meetings.

MATERIALS
- Computer, information on how to start a Cool Community campaign in your area, and the mayor's or town supervisor's phone number.

TIME
- Just a little time to visit the web site, time to review the materials, then time to meet with the mayor or town supervisor.

GLOBAL HERO 3

WE NEED MORE PEOPLE LIKE YOU IN METROPOLIS!

MAYOR

RESOURCE SAVINGS

Imagine many people in your community becoming part of the global warming solution. You truly are a Global Hero!

GLOBAL HERO RECOGNITION

Use your travel logs from each section of the journey to fill out the form below. Check off the actions that you completed and put your point total in each of the boxes marked "Global Hero Points Earned." If you have qualified, go to www.empowermentinstitute.net/globalhero and download and print a certificate recognizing your accomplishment. Congratulations!

Thanks for taking the journey. You are making a difference on our planet!

DUMPING ON GARBAGE

- ☐ No Garbage Lunches   3
- ☐ Bag Bags   1
- ☐ Wipe Swipe   1
- ☐ Gesundheit   1
- ☐ If Your Eyes Are Bigger Than Your Stomach   2
- ☐ Let It Rot   3
- ☐ Every Little Bit Helps   3
- ☐ Artist at Work   1
- ☐ Trash or Treasure   3
- ☐ Back by Popular Demand   3
- ☐ Relating to Nature: Branching Out   1

Points Needed: 12   **Global Hero Points Earned** ☐

WASTING WATER IS ALL WET

- ☐ Am I Clean Yet?   3
- ☐ Go With the Flow   2
- ☐ All Bottled Up   2
- ☐ Tanks A Lot   3
- ☐ Scrub-A-Dub Tub   2
- ☐ Scrub-A-Dub Rub   1
- ☐ Scrub-A-Dub Hub   1
- ☐ AquaCop   3
- ☐ Pearly Whites   1
- ☐ Relating to Nature: Pondering Water   1

Points Needed: 10   **Global Hero Points Earned** ☐

GETTING A CHARGE OUT OF SAVING ENERGY

- ☐ A Bright Idea   1
- ☐ Chill Out In Your Room   3
- ☐ A Fridge Physical   3
- ☐ Better a Sweater   3
- ☐ Charge It!   2
- ☐ Getting There On Your Own Steam   2
- ☐ We All Ride In a Yellow Busmarine   2
- ☐ Squash Party   2
- ☐ Shady Friends   3
- ☐ Relating to Nature: An Enlightening Experience   1

Points Needed: 12   **Global Hero Points Earned** ☐

GOOD BUYS ARE FOREVER

- ☐ What Goes Around Came Around   1
- ☐ Toxic Sleuth   3
- ☐ Leave Me a Loan   1
- ☐ Chew On This For Awhile   3
- ☐ Bulk Up   1
- ☐ When the "Gotta Have Its" Attack, Head for the Hills   2
- ☐ Vote for the Earth   3
- ☐ Vegetable Soup   2
- ☐ It Will Grow On You   3
- ☐ Relating to Nature: Second Chances   1

Points Needed: 11   **Global Hero Points Earned** ☐

WATCH OUT PLANET, HERE I COME!

- ☐ Friends for Life   3
- ☐ A Cool School   3
- ☐ Put Your Family on a Low Carbon Diet   3
- ☐ Herohood   3
- ☐ A Cool Community   3

Points Needed: 6   **Global Hero Points Earned** ☐

ABOUT THE AUTHOR

David Gershon, founder and CEO of Empowerment Institute, is one of the world's leading authorities on Earth-friendly life styles and community sustainability. His books and trainings have helped several hundred thousand people and dozens of communities develop environmentally sustainable practices.

He conceived and organized, in partnership with the United Nations Children's Fund and ABC Television, one of the planet's first major global initiatives, the First Earth Run. At the height of the Cold War, using the mythic power of relaying fire around the world, 25 million people, in partnership with the world's political leaders and media, participated in creating a profound sense of our planetary connectedness. Millions of dollars were raised for the neediest children on our planet.

David is the author of nine books including *Low Carbon Diet: A 30 Day Program to Lose 5000 Pounds.* He is currently writing *Reinventing the Social Change Formula: Social Creativity and the Practice of Empowerment.* Considered a master personal development trainer, he co-directs the Empowerment Institute Certification Program, a school for transformative change. He has lectured at Harvard, MIT, and Duke and served as an advisor to the Clinton White House and United Nations on behavior change and sustainability issues. His work has received considerable media attention and many honors.

Ever since he was a young boy, David believed we could change the world. He still believes this. This is his first children's book.

For more information visit www.empowermentinstitute.net.

CONTRIBUTORS

Steve Connolly teaches middle school math and science in Maine. He actively engages his students in principles of ecology and education through hands-on discovery. He is a storyteller for youngsters, often including environmental messages in his original tales such as, "Bert Beaver Up Ballyhac Way" and "Who Saved the Marsh?"

Dan Wetzel has been a life-long cartoonist. He had his first comic strip "Wetzel's World" published while in the sixth grade. Since then, he has created many cartoons and illustrations for newspapers, magazines and school organizations.

BOOK ORDERS

To order copies of this workbook (quantity discount available) go to: www.empowermentinstitute.net and click on "Purchase Books."

For information about the school or environmental club version of this program, visit: www.empowermentinstitute.net/lcd and click on "Cool School."